DOLLS

THE
COLLECTOR'S
CORNER

DOLLS

Grange
BOOKS

A Quantum Book

Published by Grange Books
an imprint of Grange Books Plc
The Grange
Kingsnorth Industrial Estate
Hoo, nr Rochester
Kent ME3 9ND

ISBN 1 84013 254 X

This book is produced by
Quantum Books Ltd
6 Blundell Street
London N7 9BH

Project Manager: Rebecca Kingsley
Art Director: Siân Keogh
Project Editor: Jo Wells
Designer: Martin Laurie
Editor: Lyn Coutts

The material in this publication previously appeared in *The Collector's Encyclopedia of Toys
and Dolls*, *The Collector's Book of Dolls* and *World Guide to Dolls*

QUMCCDL
Set in Gill Sans
Reproduced in Singapore by Eray Scan Pte Ltd
Printed in Singapore by Star Standard Industries (Pte) Ltd

CONTENTS

THE COLLECTOR'S GUIDE

• • • •

Dolls are now almost universally regarded as children's toys, though this is a comparatively new concept. The doll form has existed for thousands of years and in the early days of civilization 'dolls' were made as ancestor images, idols, fetishes imbued with supernatural powers, fertility symbols, talismen against evil spirits, or sometimes used in rites of magic. These often grotesque and primitive 'dolls' were made of every type of material from clay, stone and metal to leaves, beads and twigs.

It is not possible to say when dolls first became toys, but it is known that figures that were clearly dolls, modelled in clay, metal, ivory, bone and other materials, were made in Ancient Greece. There is no doubt that there were toy dolls in Europe by the Middle Ages – remains of dolls have been found in medieval graves in France. And from woodcuts, we can see that jointed dolls were made of wood, a material plentiful in the Nuremburg area of Germany, where many dolls originated.

RIGHT This fifteenth century woodcut depicts the workshop of a Nuremburg doll-maker.

By the sixteenth century dolls were being taken to America by the first colonists, as is evident from the famous coloured drawing by John White in the British Museum, London, of a naked Indian child holding a doll dressed in late Elizabethan dress.

Becoming a collector

Some people collect for investment, others find the aesthetic qualities of dolls attractive, others wish to recapture their childhood. With such a variety of dolls to choose from many collectors specialize. Some may prefer to concentrate on one type of doll, others on a particular period, maker or nationality.

The novice collector should invest time reading up on the subject; going to doll fairs, visiting museums and attending lectures. A doll club will also be a valuable source of information.

Because much of the knowledge about dolls has been pieced together relatively recently, you will sometimes come across inconsistencies. Doll factories generally did not keep archives, and knowledge of what they made previously was usually not recorded by the companies themselves. Sometimes we can only suggest a date of manufacture through knowing roughly the period during which a company operated from a specific address. A newspaper stuffed into the doll's head when new has often been the only dating evidence available.

Finding the mark

The makers' marks, usually hidden, can be incised, stamped or in relief. If they are on the back of the head, that is a fairly reliable indication

LEFT
A wooden, early English doll dated circa 1770.

FAR RIGHT
Modern celluloid
dolls dressed in
national costume.

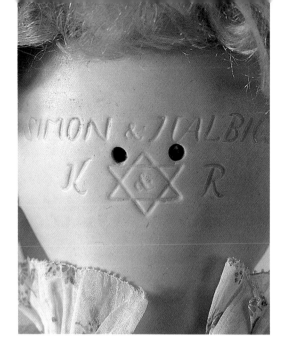

RIGHT
The maker's mark
on this doll's head
is obvious and
clear. However,
many dolls are
unmarked, making
identification more
difficult.

of origin. Marks on bodies are not quite so trustworthy, as the body could have been changed. Marks on clothing are not accurate and old clothes can easily be put on a new doll. Reproduction bisque dolls, made from a mould taken from the original, will show the original manufacturers' marks, but the reproduction artist of integrity will put his or her own signature where it can easily be seen.

In her book *Collecting Dolls*, Nora Earnshaw gives a useful summary of where to look for marks.

• Calico, muslin, composition, wood, stockinette and kid bodies – on the back or chest.

• Composition bodies – sometimes on the side or the back.

• Bisque heads – the back of the neck or the forehead.

• Composition, celluloid, wax and wax over another substance heads – marks should be regarded cautiously.

• Shoulder-plates of bisque, china, Parian, composition and celluloid – will bear marks at back or front, though the buttocks of some bisque dolls may be marked.

• Soles of the feet of some composition and kid bodies – often marked. Some makers mark the soles of shoes.

• Inside bisque, china and Parian arms or hands and on the rim inside the lower leg – incised numbers may correspond with size numbers on head and shoulder.

• Packaging (original) – check inside and out.

On an unmarked doll, the style may give a clue as to the maker – how the features are modelled and the hair is applied. But beware, a doll may have been expertly mended with marked vintage parts.

Terms, such as wax, wooden, bisque, china and so on, usually refer only to the head. To describe the whole doll terms such as 'all-bisque doll' or 'all-china doll' are used.

Fakes and reproductions

It is difficult to recognize a good fake, and there are a few about. Look out for nylon wigs (old wigs were made of real hair or mohair), new white kid bodies, clothes made of synthetic fabrics and machine-stitched clothing on old fabrics. The sewing machine came into common use in the second half of the nineteenth century. Hand-stitching is more usual on doll's clothing. In *The Collector's Encyclopaedia of Dolls*, D.E. and E. Coleman give some more clues to spotting fakes.

• Recent bisque heads have slip that is relatively free of dirt, while kiln dirt is found in antique heads.
• French bisque heads made before about 1890 were pressed. This was also true in Germany at an earlier date, especially for china heads. A pressed head has an uneven thickness and uneven interior surfaces. A poured head is smooth.
• Check the doll and clothing for signs of appropriate wear and tear and repair. Very white plaster in the eye corners of a bisque doll may mean that the eyes have been replaced.

What to look for when buying

Starting with the head examine the inside and outside. Look for firing flaws and hairline cracks. The hands should be the same colour as the head. Are the ears applied or moulded? Do firing faults or flecks of dust in the glaze spoil the overall appearance? Are there signs of flaking or chipping? What is the condition of the paint? Are the teeth original and in good condition? If the eyes are

LEFT Three glazed china heads, produced in Monte Carlo. The central head has real hair.

RIGHT An attractive collection of beautifully dressed Japanese dolls.

'sleeping' eyes, is the mechanism original and in good order? Are the clothes so tightly stitched on that you cannot examine the doll's body? Has a modern, synthetic thread been used?

Where to buy
Prices vary according to fashion and the number of dolls of a particular type on the market. If you are buying for investment, it is better to buy an inexpensive antique doll than a reproduction, however good it is.

Auctions and doll fairs are a good opportunity for buying. You may sometimes find dolls at a general antique fair. To start a collection of more recent dolls, visit fund-raising events and car boot sales.

Beware of the so called 'bargain'. You may be lucky enough to find a rare doll for a small price, but the chances are very slight. You may be buying a cracked or damaged doll or a marriage of various doll parts, all of which will significantly affect the doll's value.

CHAPTER ONE

PAPIER MÂCHÉ AND COMPOSITION DOLLS

● ● ● ●

Papier mâché (literally, chewed paper) is a paper pulp substance mixed with water, resulting in a lightweight, inexpensive mixture that can be pressed into moulds. Some form of filler is usually added, such as flour, meal, sand, clay, whiting or chalk, and the whole mixture is bound together with glue or starch paste.

The papier mâché mixture would be pressed into a mould and allowed to dry. The mould-makers, who probably worked in their own homes, would make the moulds from modelled forms. The moulds were often made in several parts and the lines on some dolls' heads will sometimes indicate how many pieces they were made from.

One-piece moulds would sometimes be used, especially for small heads. They were usually made of plaster of Paris or gypsum, and various places on the head would have to be reinforced. Linen or muslin was used as a reinforcing material. Filler and an undercoat would be used to dress the heads, and chalk, clay, gesso, gypsum or plaster were most common.

The skills of the finishers were all-important as it was upon the effects they produced that the whole doll would ultimately be judged (with the exception of the clothing). The finisher gave the doll its skin pigments, eyes, eyebrow definitions, lip and hair colouring, as well as any extra decoration. Finally, a protective coat of glue wash or varnish would be applied.

RIGHT This 1920s 'boudoir' or 'art' doll has a composition head sewn onto a cloth body. The clockwork mandolin plays music. This type of doll was intended as an adult toy.

BELOW An American made Greiner papier mâché-headed doll from circa 1850 with typical black hair parted down the middle. The head is sewn to a cloth and leather body.

RIGHT A 47cm (18½in) English papier mâché-headed doll from the late eighteenth century. Her body is made of leather and her clothes are silk.

Because paper is attractive to insects and rodents, the manufacturers tried to make it less so by adding oils and repellents and by varnishing or waxing the dolls. Both of these methods were successful in the short term, though papier mâché dolls have not lasted well over the years and those dipped in wax have cracks. Damp and excessive heat are enemies of this substance.

Papier mâché was used as a material for making votive figures in Italy in the fifteenth and sixteenth centuries. In the eighteenth century it was used for crèche figures, and for dolls a little later.

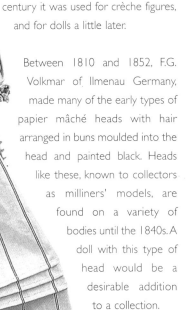

Between 1810 and 1852, F.G. Volkmar of Ilmenau Germany, made many of the early types of papier mâché heads with hair arranged in buns moulded into the head and painted black. Heads like these, known to collectors as milliners' models, are found on a variety of bodies until the 1840s. A doll with this type of head would be a desirable addition to a collection.

Mid-nineteenth century German dolls are quite different. They are child dolls with plump faces and thick necks, often with bamboo teeth and not much hair. Their bodies are made of leather and are probably French. They are filled with sawdust or straw. Charles Motschmann, famous for his dolls with limbs and bodies jointed with cloth, also made heads of papier mâché, though he progressed to heads of wood and porcelain.

In the first quarter of the nineteenth century 'Georgian wax-overs', as they are sometimes referred to, were being produced in England. These are generally regarded as wax rather than papier mâché dolls, but they had papier mâché cores. Faces were flat, and the heads are often not smooth, perhaps through warping.

Papier mâché ceased to be a popular material for dolls in Europe after the middle of the nineteenth century, but it did enjoy a revival in America. A German doll-maker named Ludwig Greiner set himself up in business in Philadelphia, and his early dolls' heads were made of paper, whiting and flour, mixed with glue and reinforced with linen. They have moulded, wavy black hair with a centre parting, painted or glass eyes and rather matronly faces. Their finish was very durable, so Greiner dolls are often found in good condition.

LEFT This French pull-string doll from circa 1905 walks, talks and blows kisses. She has a composition head and body and glass eyes and still has her original wig.

FAR LEFT This early Greiner doll has moulded hair, painted eyes, leather arms and stuffed legs. She is large – measuring 61cm (24in).

RIGHT Made of papier mâché and decorated with a rich profusion of gold fabric and glittering sequins, these rare and expensive Thai dolls are known as Monkey Dancers.

Composition

'Composition' describes modelling materials made of various substances, including plaster of Paris, bran and sawdust bound together with glue. Composition was also used as a base for wax heads, which were dipped in the wax as a means of making them more attractive yet cheaper than poured wax.

Early composition dolls had limbs made of the same material as the head, fitted to a cloth body, in the same way that shoulder-headed bisques were made. Later, the manufacturers added all-composition bodies.

The name 'M & S Superior Dolls' has been found on paper labels on composition heads produced during the 1880s and 1890s. The initials are believed to refer to the firm of Müller and Strassberger of Sonneberg. The dolls are similar in style to the Greiner dolls, with moulded hair, and tend to be blonde. The high glaze on these dolls, which was meant to be a 'superior' finish, was, in fact, thick and brittle and subject to scratching. These dolls have not survived as well as the Greiners and their faces always seem to be damaged. The glaze has usually yellowed with age.

In the early years of the 1900s, wood composition became the widely accepted material for doll-

BELOW An Effanbee Bubbles all-composition doll (circa 1925) by Fleischaker & Baum has a crying voice and an open mouth showing two teeth.

ABOVE A rare Polish soldier doll (circa 1940) measuring 48cm (19in) in its original khaki-coloured uniform. It has a papier mâché shoulder-head on a soft cloth body. The doll is thought to have been made in England.

15

making. Wood composition was a cheap material to produce, and it could be given a good finish. On one hand it was quite strong, but on the other it absorbed moisture easily which would cause the covering paint to crack.

Care and cleaning

The main disadvantage of composition as a material is that it is difficult to clean. The top coat of varnish, which most such dolls were given, can be adversely affected by water. Professionals advise rubbing – not scrubbing – soft white bread gently over the surface, which will remove the grime without injuring the doll.

It is also possible to use a liquid cleaning product, whipped into a foam and using the foam only. If you do this, test a small, inconspicuous area first. Apply the foam to a clean, soft white cloth, not to the surface of the doll, and check frequently to ensure that no colour is 'lifting'. Use a different section of the cloth each time you apply it. Do not soak the doll. Rinse off the foam with a cloth slightly moistened in distilled water.

Papier mâché and composition dolls should be examined for signs of infestation by insects and the use of an insecticide in storage is advisable. Store the dolls in a dry place in an even temperature. If you wrap them, use an acid-free tissue paper.

The faces of papier mâché and composition dolls are often found with chipped noses and rubbed areas. Unfortunately, there is not much to be done about this, but some dextrous doll-owners have successfully used plastic wood to repair chips.

CHAPTER TWO

WOODEN DOLLS

● ● ● ●

Wooden dolls or doll forms have been made world-wide since early times. Recognizable doll figures have been found in the Nile Valley preserved by the hot, dry climate of that area. These figures are among the earliest wooden 'dolls' to survive.

Wooden dolls turned on a lathe by woodworkers have also been in existence for many years, and the skittle shape produced by this method is seen again and again, in the dolls of primitive tribes and particularly in the stiff bodies of the seventeenth and eighteenth century English woodens.

'Queen Anne' dolls

Among the most sought after wooden dolls are the 'Queen Anne', or 'Queen Anne-type' dolls. In fact some of these pre-date Queen Anne (who ruled England between 1702 and 1714), and others were made well into the nineteenth century. They are associated with England. Although examples are quite often found in the United States, they were probably taken there by the early settlers. It is fairly certain that the 'Queen Anne-type' doll had its birth and adolescence in the UK.

These dolls had bodies turned on a lathe, with hand-carved heads and painted eyes or black, enamelled eyes without pupils; sometimes the eyes were blue. The head and body was

RIGHT This wooden Queen Anne-type doll (circa early 1800s) has a stump-type, one-piece body and jointed wooden limbs. The wig base is nailed to the head.

BELOW Three
rare Thuringian
nursing dolls
(1700s). When
the string is pulled,
the arms move up
and down, rocking
the baby. The
23cm (9in) skittle
shape is made by
turning the dolls
on a lathe.

carved from one piece of wood to form a stump, and the head was finished with gesso and varnish and delicate face painting. The fingers and hands of these dolls were finely-carved and gesso-covered and were attached to the body with cloth and a pin. The legs were carved and jointed and set into grooves at the base of the torso; they often had well-defined calves and ankles. The dolls were made with a high breast form.

The eyebrows on the earlier dolls were the so-called 'stitched' variety, which are produced by a series of little black dots. The wig was tacked or nailed onto the doll's head, and sometimes a black 'patch' – which was then considered to be a sign of beauty – was seen on the cheek.

With their painted eyes, red cheeks, prim painted mouths and beauty spots, many of the late seventeenth century and early eighteenth century dolls bear a striking resemblance to each other, and to Lady Clapham, the famous doll which, along with Lord Clapham, is exhibited in the Victoria and Albert Museum, London.

ABOVE This French doll (1700s) from the Galéa collection has a beautifully carved, painted face, coated with gesso The hands are finely shaped.

The basic skittle shape can also be seen in the turned wooden dolls of the Ertzgebirge, Germany. Some of these quite simple doll figures are fitted with arms that move when a string is pulled, so that the bundle in the doll's arms representing her baby, can be rocked to sleep.

It is interesting to see this skittle shape recurring in more modern times. It can be seen for example, in the wooden shoe doll from the Edinburgh Museum of Childhood, in the nesting matriochkas dolls from Russia, and in the kokeshis of Japan. Modern versions of the stump doll also appear from time to time, made by craftspeople.

Grödnertals and penny woodens

All these dolls were overtaken in popularity by the wooden, jointed 'Grödnertals'. Then came the penny woodens, the so-called 'Dutch' dolls and the peg woodens. They came unclothed, which made them ideal playthings, and this was the type of doll Queen Victoria played with as a girl between 1831 and 1833. Most of these dolls were dressed as ladies of the nobility and all were given titles by the young princess, while the smaller group represented the famous ballet dancers and opera singers she would have seen at the theatre.

The early Grödnertals degenerated in the latter part of the century, which is not surprising since they were turned out in their hundreds, and sold by the dozen.

In her book *The Collectors' History of Dolls*, Constance Eileen King distinguishes between the various types of peg doll. It is in the treatment of the head that the greatest difference between the Grödnertal and the early penny woodens lies. The latter have simple round heads with the hair painted on, whereas the earlier dolls had hairstyles that involved carving and ornamentation.

These are the best known of the wooden dolls, but folk dolls were made in Sweden, England and Russia as well as in Germany. Folk dolls were also made in the United States out of pine wood, but Joel Ellis of Springfield, Vermont, is credited with updating the wooden peg-jointed doll.

ABOVE This carved oak figure (circa 1600s) is holding a bottle and glass. It was carved directly out of a piece of oak.

LEFT Also known as Bristle dolls, these moulded dough or composition Piano doll figures are only 6cm (2¹/₂in) high. Their bodies are supported by four bristles, and when they are placed on a piano and it vibrates, their hanging, articulated legs 'dance'.

19

Ellis dolls are rare and expensive and they are not often found in Europe. Collectors stand a better chance of finding a Schoenhut doll at a reasonable price because they were exported to France, Germany and Britain.

The Schoenhut dolls are complicated pieces of work, with a mechanism of steel spring hinges, double spring tension and swivel connections. This meant that the dolls could be placed in natural positions. They were made entirely of wood, with no rubber cord. They were painted with enamel oil colours and stood firmly on posts that fitted into the soles of the feet and onto a metal disc. Schoenhut dolls came in 60 different styles. Some dolls had carved and painted hair, and others had ribbons and hats. Some had painted eyes, and others had glass eyes.

The All Wood Perfection Art Dolls were an instant success. They were sturdy, aesthetically pleasing (the heads were carved by Graziano, one of the best-known sculptors of the time) and attractively dressed.

Since the invention of plastics and vinyl, few firms bother to produce wooden dolls and in the latter part of the twentieth century it is left to a few artist craftspeople to continue this tradition. The Swiss and German husband and wife team of Abhinavo and Regina Sandreuter have created superb wooden models of children with articulated bodies made of eight wooden parts joined by elastic string held by wooden dowels. The heads and limbs are modelled in clay by the artists, then cast and mechanically produced in maple wood, the fine detail of each doll being hand-carved by the artists.

LEFT A rare eighteenth century doll in French costume. His head, lower arms and lower legs are made of wood. The rest of the doll is made of stuffed fabric.

FAR LEFT Eric Horne's traditional jointed wooden peg dolls range from 46cm (18in) to 6mm (¹/₄in.) All the dolls, except the two smallest sizes, are fully jointed and pegged with wooden pins.

21

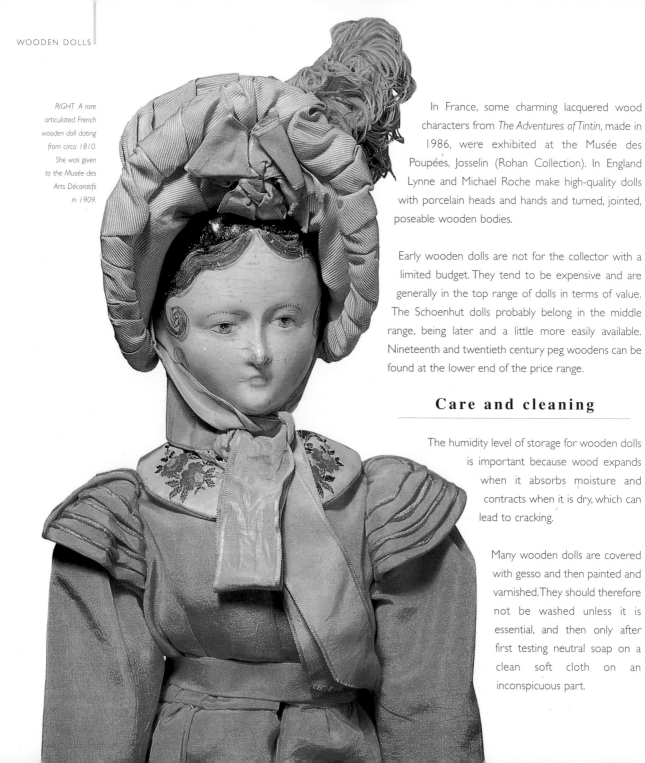

In France, some charming lacquered wood characters from *The Adventures of Tintin*, made in 1986, were exhibited at the Musée des Poupées, Josselin (Rohan Collection). In England Lynne and Michael Roche make high-quality dolls with porcelain heads and hands and turned, jointed, poseable wooden bodies.

Early wooden dolls are not for the collector with a limited budget. They tend to be expensive and are generally in the top range of dolls in terms of value. The Schoenhut dolls probably belong in the middle range, being later and a little more easily available. Nineteenth and twentieth century peg woodens can be found at the lower end of the price range.

Care and cleaning

The humidity level of storage for wooden dolls is important because wood expands when it absorbs moisture and contracts when it is dry, which can lead to cracking.

Many wooden dolls are covered with gesso and then painted and varnished. They should therefore not be washed unless it is essential, and then only after first testing neutral soap on a clean soft cloth on an inconspicuous part.

CHAPTER THREE

WAX DOLLS

• • • •

rom medieval times, wax was established in Europe as an artistic medium; funeral effigies and floral displays were often made in wax. By the eighteenth century, it was an established doll material throughout Europe and America.

Wax dolls are certainly among the most beautiful dolls available to the collector. Wax as a medium gives rich, authentically natural skin tones with a translucent quality that cannot be achieved in bisque. As a soft medium, of course, wax was subject to damage and destruction and many examples have not survived. Prior to the early 1800s, the dolls were sometimes eaten by mice, until the manufacturers added an ingredient to make the wax less desirable to rodents. Some wax dolls melted when left by the fire and others were sat upon.

LEFT A wax doll of the young Queen Victoria, produced in the 1970s by the artist Margaret Glover, based on a print of the Queen.

Because of their vulnerability, few very early wax dolls exist, though the Bethnal Green Museum of Childhood in London does have a 20cm (8in) 1754 wax doll that belonged to a Laetitia Clark. She started a family tradition of dressing dolls in the fashion of the day, so that there is a series of these dolls from 1754 to 1910.

ABOVE This late-nineteenth century Pierotti baby was made in England circa 1885. The delicate features are typical of this type of poured wax doll. The body is made of stuffed cloth and the lower limbs are also wax.

Contrary to popular belief, wax dolls will not melt simply in a warm room, but if left in a sunny window exposed wax may become quite white.

Method of manufacture

To make a wax head, a sculpture would be made from which a mould would be taken. This was warmed and the liquid wax was then poured in – sometimes in two or three stages to get the right thickness. White lead and carmine would sometimes be added for colour and, when set, the mould would be taken off and the finishing touches put to the doll. Eye holes would be cut for insertion of the glass eyes, eyelashes would be added and the hair fixed in clumps into the wax of the head. The head would then be dusted with potato starch, a powdered alabaster or pumice to give a good complexion. After this, the cheeks were tinted with rouge and the lips and nostrils

touched with vermillion. Holes were made in the breastplate of the doll's head so that it could be sewn onto the cloth body. In the same way, the limbs were fashioned and sewn on.

Dipped wax dolls

Wax is an expensive material and when mass production started in the mid-nineteenth century, ways had to be found to cheapen manufacture, for example by using a papier mâché core and wax-dipping it to limit the amount of wax needed.

Papier mâché core dolls' heads would sometimes be glued to the body. The wax on the poured wax dolls varies in colour from a very hot pink through the various flesh tones to pale pink. Only the early, almost pure beeswax dolls have a tell-tale yellowish complexion. Unfortunately, over the years the dolls with a heavy dusting of pumice may have turned a dirty-looking grey colour, as the layer of pumice solidified and then discoloured. This can prove difficult to remove and should be left to the experts.

25

Slit-head dolls

These early dolls, made from wax-over-papier mâché, often have just a slit in the top of the head – hence their nickname – through which the hair is distributed and then glued down and formed into ringlets. Some are also found with a hole cut at the back of the head with a papier mâché plate fixed over it, evidently to enable the eyes to be secured. This is usually waxed over and the wig glued over that.

The glass eyes in wax dolls made before 1850 were without pupils and were very dark, almost black in colour. Some examples have moving eyes which were opened and shut by means of a wire coming out of the body at the waistline. These were probably introduced around 1825. Eyebrow details were usually painted onto the papier mâché before dipping. Wax dolls are often found with extremely crazed faces. The seasonal expansion and contraction of the papier mâché layer beneath the wax would have caused the wax to crack all over the surface.

The bodies, legs and feet of these slit-head dolls are crudely stuffed, the feet usually turning inwards giving a pigeon-toed effect; the arms are usually made of leather. Curiously, the dolls with brown leather arms usually have only three fingers on each hand; while those with white kid arms have the usual five.

LEFT A poured wax doll created as a portrait of the actress Lillie Langtry, mistress of Edward VII. She has bright blue eyes and a clear complexion. This particular doll was given to an employee of the famous lady, who in turn donated the keepsake to the owner of the Lilliput Museum, England.

LEFT This French doll (circa 1870) is an example of wax-over-papier mâché.

The most striking feature of all is the amazing smile on these dolls' faces; almost every example smiles as if she has been keeping an amusing secret for over 100 years.

ABOVE *Edward is wax throughout. He was made by the well-known modern doll-maker Gillie Charlson in Lancashire, England.*

Poured wax dolls

The majority of the best pure wax dolls were made in England and many examples by the most well-known names, among them Pierotti, Montanari, Marsh, Meech and Peck, are with us today. Most of the 'poured wax' dolls, which is the name given to wax dolls without papier mâché cores, are

LEFT A poured wax model of Queen Victoria as a young woman in her Coronation robes, purchased at the Great Exhibition of 1851 and kept under a glass dome.

FAR LEFT An exquisite portrait – in poured wax – of Queen Victoria's granddaughter Princess Louise on her wedding day.

unmarked and most collectors will refer to a 'Pierotti-type' doll or a 'Montanari-type' doll because they cannot be identified with any degree of certainty. In extremely rare cases, a Montanari doll may be found bearing a signature in brownish ink on the lower left hand corner of the torso. The marked Pierotti dolls, with the name scratched roughly onto the back of the doll's head are rare.

Wax dolls were also made in France, and in the mid-nineteenth century Sonneberg in Germany was famous for them. These heads were usually reinforced with plaster. Fritz Bartenstein (1880–98) was particularly

LEFT A modern (1970s) wax doll by the British artist Margaret Glover.

29

famous for his double-faced doll, one side laughing and the other crying. The head could be turned by the movement of a string, and one of the faces would be hidden by a hood.

Other early wax-over-papier mâché dolls include the so-called 'pumpkin head' dolls with fancy moulded hairstyles, stuffed bodies and wooden limbs. Not to be forgotten in this area are the charming little wax-over-papier mâché 'bonnet head' dolls with moulded hats, often with three plumes in the front.

By 1904, very few wax dolls were being made in Sonneberg, and England was the only country where

RIGHT A rare Dutch doll measuring only 5.5cm (2¼in). He is made of solid wax and sits in a high chair, holding a flower in his hand.

BELOW Two German dolls with solid wax heads and limbs. They depict members of the British monarchy – the Prince of Wales (right) and the Princess Royal (left) – and were probably souvenirs.

BELOW Crèche figures were made for religious purposes. This rare German figure, dating from circa 1780 has a wax head and carved wooden hands.

they continued to be popular. The German companies of Kestner and Kämmer & Reinhardt also made wax dolls and, in fact, the famous Kämmer & Reinhardt 'Mein Liebling' ('My Darling') doll was also made in wax. By 1920, wax dolls were being used popularly for display and costume purposes. In 1925, in Paris, Mme T. Lazarski made display dolls of similar form to the English examples. The dolls featured in publicity material and in movies. Wax dolls were also made by the leading manufacturers as display mannequins for shop windows.

ABOVE Two solid wax dolls dating from circa 1924. They were probably made for advertising clothes.

31

ABOVE A German wax doll dating from circa 1880. She is still wearing her original clothes and still has her original hair. The glass eyes are fixed.

BELOW Two mid-nineteenth century German wax-over-composition dolls. The larger doll is a 'pumpkin head' with a broad face and a head that is flat from back to front.

Care and cleaning

• Avoid exposure to strong sunlight or other sources of direct heat.

• Inspect where the body joins the head regularly, as the glue will contract with age and the calico fabric rot.

• Clean wax with a little cold cream on a smooth, white cloth, avoiding painted features. Wipe on the cold cream, then using the clean section of cloth, wipe it off gently.

• Never put a plastic bag in contact with wax as the condensation will affect the texture of the wax. Instead, use white or natural pure silk or fine white lawn.

BELOW A two-faced doll produced by Fritz Bartenstein of Germany circa 1880. The head turns round to reveal a crying face. The body is wax-over-papier mâché.

CHAPTER FOUR

CHINA AND PARIAN DOLLS

• • • •

A china doll is one with a head made of glazed porcelain. These were made mostly in Germany from about 1840, but there are also some very desirable Danish heads, made by the Royal Copenhagen factory, and French heads, produced by Huret, Rohmer and Barrois among others, which were the forerunners of the Parisiennes or fashion dolls. The prestigious firms of Meissen and Königliche Porzellanmanufaktur in Berlin also produced china heads. Those from the latter are known for the richness of their glaze and the sensitive modelling of their faces.

China dolls were produced from around 1830, and represented men, women and children in glazed porcelain. Production continued well into the 1900s. Knowledge of chinas is scant, which makes dating difficult.

As with papier mâché dolls, heads were often sold alone for the bodies to be made by mothers or nursemaids. China heads on their own are quite commonly found and are now extremely collectable. Most chinas are unmarked so a marked head is highly collectable.

The bodies of china dolls vary considerably. Some were sold to shops which supplied them to private buyers for pincushions

LEFT A German pink lustre china-headed doll dating from circa 1860. The hair is moulded with a centre parting and curls over her ears.

RIGHT A glazed china doll with pink cheeks and blue eyes, made in Germany circa 1860. Her arms are made of pale leather.

ABOVE A 35.5cm (14in) German
Parian pedlar doll with leather arms
and glass eyes and blonde,

moulded hair. She probably dates from
circa 1850. Gloves, purses, beads, laces
and buttons are on display in her tray.

and other artistic knick-knacks as well as dolls,
others were given bodies by outworkers. The bodies
were mostly stuffed with sawdust and given porcelain
or leather lower limbs, but there are many examples
of china dolls with wooden bodies.

After about 1860, these popular dolls became
cheaper and more stylized. A great many 'Frozen
Charlottes' (also called Bathing Dolls) were made.

These are stiff little white or pink glazed dolls with pillar legs and black moulded hair.

Later china dolls were more child-like, with chubby faces, short necks and lower foreheads. The sloping shoulders of the early dolls were replaced by smaller, squarer ones.

Some blonde china dolls were made. Some heads were given a pink lustre finish, others had glass eyes and were made without hair so that a wig could be added. These often have a black spot painted on the top of the head, though the reason for this is not known.

Unglazed china dolls, were often cast from the same moulds as the glazed dolls. The bisques, as they are called, are usually blonde.

In the late nineteenth century bonnet dolls appeared. One fanciful group of these, known as the Marguerites, wore hats in the shape of flowers and butterflies. Many of these can be found in the U.S.A.

Hairstyles and ornament

Many people collect chinas for their different hairstyles, and there is an almost limitless variety, including braided coronets, snoods, centre partings, exposed ears with a bun at the back (like the young Queen Victoria), spaniel

LEFT A fine dolls head produced by the German Meissen factory circa 1840. The combination of dark hair and blue eyes in this doll is unusual.

ABOVE A China doll from Emma Clear in Los Angeles circa 1940. This doll, named Danny Boy, was one of the few originals produced.

ears-style flaring at the sides, and the painted wagon-style with centre parting and 13 curls around the face ending at the neck. This attention to detail and to fashion, along with ornamental exotic features were clearly an attempt by manufacturers to woo customers. Nothing has been left untried. Trims of every kind and colour were moulded onto the heads.

Such a wide range of chinas exists that one can only assume that they were very popular. Their durability must have made them attractive, for although they were breakable they could be washed by their owners and did not scratch or lose their colour.

Methods of manufacture

There were two methods of making glazed china heads. One was to roll out the clay and press it into a plaster of Paris mould; the other was to mix the clay with water until it was liquid and could be poured. This 'slip' was then poured into the mould, where it was left until

RIGHT China doll heads from the late nineteenth century with black moulded hair. The sew holes are for attaching the heads to the bodies.

much of the moisture had been absorbed by the plaster. The surplus 'slip' was then poured off, leaving behind a perfect impression.

The head moulds were usually made in two halves which, when they were 'leather hard', were joined together with more 'slip'. When the whole head was dry, the joins had to be 'ferried' so that no line was left to spoil the look of the finished head. (A head mould can also be made in three or more pieces, for a finer finish.) After that, it was a question of bisque-firing the heads and then painting and overglazing them or glazing them and firing once again with on-glaze enamels.

Nowadays, studio potters seem to concentrate on either making their own bisque beads or making bisque reproductions of the famous designs of the last century, but in the 1940s a craftswoman named Emma Clear started to make reproduction glazed china dolls, basing her first on a Jenny Lind doll of the 1850s. Altogether she created about 40 different limited edition dolls.

Parian dolls

Parian is a form of fine bisque porcelain. Though there is dispute over whether or not the white bisque dolls we know were true Parian, they are attractive to collectors. So-called Parian doll heads, which are usually blonde, were made in Germany from about 1850 to 1880 and were sold without bodies, like the china heads. In fact, some Parians were made from the moulds used for china dolls and they do resemble them.

LEFT Glazed Meissen dolls from the KPM factory in Berlin circa 1837.

The definition of the features of a Parian is more marked than that of the chinas. The painting is subtle and attractive and the dolls usually have blue eyes. The bodies vary, home-made types to commercially-made cloth bodies with Parian or leather arms.

Identifying and naming

Collectors have devised a way of identifying the usually unmarked Parian dolls, giving them names, some of which are shared with chinas. Dolly Madison (1870–80), Countess Dagmar, with blonde and black hair (1870), Empress Eugénie, Princess Alexandra, Alice in Wonderland, Jenny Lind (1870), Highland Mary, and Adelina Patti are among the best known.

However, certain heads are found only on Parians, as if they were produced either by a different manufacturer or the design lent itself more readily to Parian. Generally

ABOVE. A German
Parian doll,
produced circa
1864 that was
exported to
America and won
a prize at an
exhibition in 1959.

Glass eyes are also to be found on Parian dolls and are the most highly sought-after of the type, commanding high prices. Some of the most prized Parians have elaborately moulded frills on their shoulder plates and exquisite hair ornamentation. Another doll not found in china is the 'Blue scarf' doll which is said to represent the Empress Louise of Prussia. These dolls have been reproduced by Emma Clear between 1940 and 1950 and are marked with her name and the year.

Care and cleaning

A glazed china doll is as prone to wear and tear as a bisque doll and it should never be scrubbed with harsh abrasives or detergents. If the colour has been added as an on-glaze after the firing of the main transparent glaze, hard rubbing can easily cause the colour, particularly if it is lustre, to disappear. If the colour has been applied as an underglaze, it will be somewhat protected by the shiny transparent glaze.

As with all cleaning, proceed slowly and carefully. Place the doll on a padded surface, such as an old towel. Use a neutral detergent whipped to a foam. Clean an inconspicuous area first as a test, using the foam on cotton wool swabs. Rinse off with a soft white cloth that has been moistened with warm, distilled water. You can clean Parian and bisque dolls in the same way.

All paint reacts to light, pollution and strong detergents and all china and bisque is liable to damage caused by careless handling and prolonged, harsh exposure.

speaking, there are far more elaborately decorated Parian dolls in existence than china ones. Parian versions of Empress Eugénie are sometimes referred to as Lucy. Her wonderful head with its silver-white feather and purple lustre tassel has an exquisitely moulded, firmly structured face.

BISQUE DOLLS

• • • •

As mentioned earlier, china-headed dolls were replaced by white bisque (Parian) dolls with white lower limbs and blonde hair. These in turn changed in the 1860s and 1870s into coloured bisque heads of a rounder, more realistic type.

The third, and for many collectors, the most important type of ceramic dolls are those with bisque heads and limbs. Bisque is made from the same substance as china, but it is unglazed. After an initial firing at a very high temperature the facial painting is carried out, and the bisque is then fired again, this time at a lower temperature. Such painting is sometimes known as 'fired in bisque'.

Bisque was the material most favoured by the great French and German doll-makers, and it remained a favourite material for the creation of dolls' heads from the mid-nineteenth century until the 1930s.

Bisque proved to be an extraordinarily versatile material, and the second half of the nineteenth century saw a tremendous range of designs and treatments of dolls, which were created to represent women, children and babies, men and boys. The heads were modified from the previously used shoulderhead or swivel neck to socket and flange necks. Eyes were painted, then glass, later sleeping or 'googly'. It is only in recent years that bisque has been superseded by vinyl.

LEFT Two Parisienne dolls produced in France circa 1860. They are dressed in contemporary Paris fashion and were sold with a full complement of accessories.

RIGHT A french
doll produced in
the late
nineteenth
century. She is
probably an
unmarked Jumeau
doll. This doll has a
bisque head,
hands and arms.

RIGHT A french doll produced in the late nineteenth century. She is probably an unmarked Jumeau doll. This doll has a bisque head, hands and arms.

Matt finish bisque-headed fashion dolls, or Parisiennes as they are called, were a speciality of the French doll-makers, some of which made their own heads while others continued to import the heads from Germany and employed outworkers to make and dress the leather bodies. Jumeau, Rohmer, Huret and Gaultier were among those who made their own heads as well as bodies, but not all of their dolls are signed. A beautifully dressed Parisienne is a prized treasure in any collection. Among the names to look for are those mentioned above and Barrois, Simonne, E. Denamaur, Schmitt & Fils, A. Thuillier, Bru and Jules Steiner.

Jumeau bébés

The firm of Jumeau was established in 1842, but from 1877 onwards it was the giant among doll-makers, winning gold and silver medals at international exhibitions. Jumeau continued to make fashion dolls up to the end of the century and experimented with different types of body.

Jumeau also made a completely different type of doll named the bébé, which represents a child about eight years of age. The bébé was not strictly their invention; Jules Steiner and Bru had developed it earlier.

The bébé had a different type of body. Instead of the gussetted kid leather body stuffed with sawdust, bodies were made of wood and ball-jointed, which made them expensive. Later, they were made of composition, which lowered the cost. By 1881 Jumeau had sold 85,000.

LEFT A doll on a stick made by Ernst Heubach of Koppelsdorf, Germany circa 1900. When it is moved around on its stick music plays.

41

very lovely faces, swivel necks on a shoulderplate and a cork plate and they are marked with a crescent and circle or sometimes with a circle and dot. Some later Bru dolls have wooden, ball-jointed arms and legs.

F. G. Gaultier is another maker of fine bisque heads. He patented a method of cutting out and inserting glass eyes in bisque heads. The Lanternier factory of Limoges made some lively looking bisque-headed dolls, but of varying quality.

BELOW A pair of rare bisque Parisienne-type dolls dressed in French regional costume, dated circa 1870. They are dressed for their wedding.

The Bru company's aim was to produce high-quality dolls. As a result its output was smaller than that of Jumeau. Among its innovations were double-faced dolls, walking and talking dolls, and 'Le Dormeur', which could open and close its eyelids.

Early Bru dolls have pink or white kid bodies and articulated porcelain or wooden limbs. The bébés have

Formation of the SFBJ

By the end of the nineteenth century, German doll-makers had perfected their mass-production methods and were exporting cheap but strong dolls with jointed composition bodies and bisque heads.

In order to combat this growing competition, in 1898 French doll-makers joined together and formed the Société Française de Fabrication de Bébés et Jouets (SFBJ).

Moulds that had been used previously by the individual members of the company were later re-used. As a result there is often a strong resemblance between SFBJ dolls and early Bru and Jumeau dolls. In fact, a marked SFBJ doll may also have a Jumeau or another maker's stamp on it.

By 1922 SFBJ had an output of several million dolls a year. This prolific production means that collectors today are still able to purchase a wide range of SFBJ dolls of every sort and every quality.

ABOVE A French SFBJ doll wearing a fashionable costume, dated circa 1925. This doll has a bisque head and a compostion body.

German doll-makers

From the middle of the nineteenth century to the early part of the twentieth century, the German doll-makers dominated the world market. They were situated for the most part in the district of Thuringia in southern Germany, where there were natural resources of wood and china clay and plenty of labour.

The doll-making firms clustered together, exchanging ideas, making good use of each others' skills. Mass production was carried out on an assembly-line basis, and a large proportion was exported. Most of the world's children played with German dolls until the First World War.

BELOW A group of German character dolls. The two large dolls (circa 1909) were produced by Kammer and Reinhardt. The others are dated circa 1914. The winking doll is probably by Kestner.

The firm of Armand Marseille was the most prolific of all German doll-makers. Because of its high rate of production its dolls can be found easily by collectors and at a reasonable price. Among its huge range of dolls (which are usually marked 'A.M.' and/or 'Armand Marseille' and 'Germany') were its Dream Babies, Floradoras, googly-eyed dolls and Orientals.

After the little girl dolls came the fashion for baby dolls, with baby-like faces, and bent-limbed bodies and character dolls, which resembled real babies.

BELOW A trio of realistic-looking German bisque dolls produced in the late nineteenth to early twentieth century.

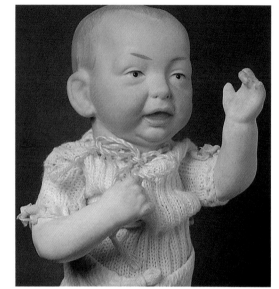

ABOVE *Kammer and Reinhardt produced this bisque baby doll circa 1908. This company* *was the first German manufacturer to attempt to make a life-like baby doll with an expression on its face.*

From 1886 to 1909, the firm of Kämmer & Reinhardt had made only dolly-faced dolls. Then, inspired by the realism of the New Art Dolls of Munich, it made the first of its long line of successful character dolls.

The Kämmer & Reinhardt dolls are very appealing. The best-known models are the so-called 'Kaiser baby', those made in mould 101 (known as Peter and Marie) and the Hans and Gretchen dolls.

Simon & Halbig was another long-established Thuringian porcelain manufacturer, second only in size to Armand

Marseille. A great many German doll-makers and some French ones, including Jumeau and other members of the SFBJ, used Simon & Halbig heads from about 1900.

The firm of J. D. Kestner was the only German doll manufacturer to make both heads and bodies and one of the first to manufacture dressed dolls. Founded in 1816, it produced papier mâché and wooden dolls, acquiring a porcelain factory in 1860 and making glazed porcelain doll's heads. Its dolls are considered to be of the highest quality.

Confusion surrounds the name of Heubach, since there were two quality doll-makers working at about the same time, Gebrüder Heubach of Lichte and Ernst Heubach of Köppelsdorf. The son of Armand Marseille had married the daughter of Ernst Heubach and as a result in 1919 the porcelain factories of Marseille and Heubach merged to become the Köppelsdorfer Porzellanfabrik.

LEFT A Simon and Halbig doll holding a teddy bear. She was probably made circa 1899 in Germany. The body is pink leather and the head bisque.

ABOVE The German company Armand Marseille produced this bisque doll (AM 390) circa 1925. She has a composition body.

45

RIGHT An all-bisque reproduction Kestner character baby produced in 1983, probably in England.

ABOVE Realism reaches its peak in this 1990s English bisque doll. Lynne and Michael Roche of Bath, UK made this doll – Sophy – based on a photograph of the French writer Colette as a child.

A Schoenau & Hoffmeister doll can be quite easily confused with a doll from Simon & Halbig, because the companies had the same initials. Both firms used a star mark on some of their dolls' heads; heads made by Simon & Halbig for Kämmer & Reinhardt, for example, are sometimes marked with a star with a 'K' and 'R' on either side and the 'S & W' underneath. Schoenau and Hoffmeister are also sometimes marked with a star with a 'PB' in the centre and the initials 'S' and 'H' on either side.

The Handwercks (Max and Heinrich), Cüno & Otto Dressle, Fritz Bartenstein, Theodor Recknagel, Hermann Steiner and Kley & Hahn are just a few of the dozens of German doll manufacturers that were supplying dolls during the late 1800s and early 1900s.

British ceramic dolls

British bisque dolls have not been highly-rated in the past, but there are some worth collecting if only for their interest value. When the First World War cut off the supply of German bisque dolls to the U.K., the Staffordshire potteries were encouraged to make 'pot' dolls using an inferior type of clay, which is usually known as British ceramic, and often using moulds made from existing German dolls.

By 1917 about 100 factories were producing dolls in the United Kingdom, though not on a large scale. They had British ceramic heads and bodies of white kid, cloth or composition. The Diamond Pottery Co. Ltd. of

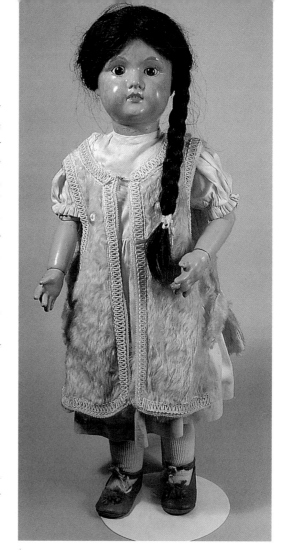

LEFT The English company Nunn and Smeed made jointed dolls during World War I, when German imports stopped. This Dolly Dimple doll has a British ceramic head and a composition body.

Hanley, Staffordshire, was one such company, producing some heavy doll's heads of pinkish hue. The Doll Pottery Co. of Fenton, Staffordshire, also made a variety of dolls and dolls' heads. Hancock & Sons and Hewitt & Leadbeater of Longton, Staffordshire (manufacturers of porcelain crest china), were among those that began making dolls at the outbreak of the war.

BELOW Two
American bisque
dolls produced by
Effanbee, based
on the movie star
John Wayne.

The firm of Nunn & Smeed of Liverpool manufactured jointed dolls with a new finish for bodies that looked like porcelain and was waterproof and non-toxic. In 1921 the company took out a patent for the 'Nunsuch' walking doll.

W. Speight of Dewsbury started business manufacturing hair pieces and theatrical wigs, but it later went on to produce a range of ceramic-headed dolls with names such as Dinkie, Dazzle Dazzle and Kidette Classic fully-jointed dolls.

American bisque doll-makers

American firms, such as Horsman and Borgfeldt, imported great quantities of dolls from Germany and France, but they also commissioned American artists to design dolls specifically for the American market. The Horsman Campbell Kids were inspired by advertising characters for a soup and their HEbees and SHEbees were based on drawings by Charles Twelvetrees.

Borgfeldt commissioned designer Grace Drayton, who is known best for her googly-eyed dolls, to design dolls for him. The company also commissioned Grace Storey Putnam, who created the famous Bye-Lo Baby, the Million-Dollar Baby. Grace Storey Putnam modelled this doll from a real-life baby and it turned out to be a huge commercial success.

Caring for bisque dolls

The same rules apply to cleaning bisque dolls as for cleaning china dolls. The paint on a doll's face may have been fired on, but it is still vulnerable to harsh treatment. In some cases, the colour may not have been fired on and then it is even more important not to wash with harsh detergents or to scrub.

CHAPTER SIX

CLOTH DOLLS

• • • •

From a child's point of view, the warmth and cuddliness of cloth dolls makes them especially attractive. Cloth, or rag, dolls have been with us since the earliest times: they have been found in the ancient tombs of Peru and Egypt.

A rag doll was always an affordable toy. It could be either home-made or commercially-produced and was within reach of both rich and poor. Some cloth dolls were made purely as playthings, others were produced for promotional purposes. Promotional dolls are a collecting field in themselves and include such dolls as 'Rastus, Cream of Wheat Chef' (1922) or the two-piece rag dolls Kelloggs' 'Goldilocks and the Mama Bear' (1917–18) designed by Lela Fellom and the 'Aunt Jemima' doll (1923–1925).

Certain companies' names spring to mind when considering cloth dolls, among them Käthe Kruse and Lenci, both have an inspiring history of manufacture and are still in

LEFT Two cloth dolls with felt faces by Norah Wellings of England, represent women in the armed services during World War II.

RIGHT An early woven doll from Peru dating from the first century AD. It was recovered from a child's tomb.

business today. Such names as Steiff, Chad Valley, Deans Rag Book Company and Nora Wellings were also in the forefront. Besides the products of these well-known firms, there are numerous cloth dolls and advertising dolls from unknown sources.

Käthe Kruse

Käthe Kruse used her own children as models for her realistic dolls. Her first dolls were made for her children. Her early commissioned dolls were made in Berlin (from 1910) and the later ones in Bavaria.

To make the dolls, the head was first sculpted and a mould taken. The shape of the head was made from stiffened muslin, sprayed with fixative and painted. In the early dolls the finely-grained muslin was visible.

The early Käthe Kruse dolls have appealingly sad faces, and it is said

LEFT A German doll with a cloth body, produced by Käthe Kruse circa 1925. She is dressed in Dutch national costume, complete with clogs.

ABOVE Kathe Kruse, a German artist, used her own children as models for her dolls. The heads were made of painted, stiffened muslin, the bodies were layers of cotton, wound around a frame. These two are typical examples of her work.

that she made them like that to reflect the sadness of the First World War years. These dolls were not cheap to begin with and they command good prices today, particularly the earlier ones. Her dolls are signed Käthe Kruse on the left foot and are marked with a serial number. This was a coded control number system from which the age of the doll can be ascertained. Between 1945 and 1951, the right foot bore the stamp 'Made in Germany US Zone'.

Until 1928, Käthe Kruse dolls had loosely sewn-on heads; the turned head was first produced in 1929. From 1910 to 1929 they all had painted hair after which

RIGHT A cloth boudoir doll from 1920s
or '30s France. She has a pressed fabric
head and composition hands.

ABOVE A cloth
doll produced by
the English firm
Chad Valley circa
1930. He is based
on a cartoon
character from a
daily newspaper
the Daily Mirror.

LEFT A 1920s boudoir doll, probably produced in France. She has a cloth body and pressed fabric face and is over 1m (41in) tall. This type of doll was produced for adults.

ABOVE The French doll artist Michele Lepinay makes dolls of stuffed cotton. She made small quantities for five or six years in the 1980s.

ABOVE A sleeping baby doll, designed by Kathe Kruse to help to teach new mothers the art of childcare in Germany circa 1925.

real hair wigs were introduced and became very popular, although the painted hair examples still continued. The eyes were almost always painted, and all dolls had closed mouths.

It is interesting to note that from 1910 to 1956 only five different doll head types were produced, with slight variations as well as different numbers and names. The first head was merely called No. I, second was 'Schlenkerchen' ('The Little Dawdler') – Doll No.II 'Trämerchen' ('The Little Dreamer') and 'Du Mein' ('You mine'). Dolls numbered V and VI were next (III and IV did not exist.) 'Deutsches Kind' ('German Child') was Doll No. VIII and 'Hämpelchen' was Doll No. XII. After the 1957 model, Hanne Kruse dolls came into existence. Käthe Kruse dolls were also produced in celluloid. The firm's financial crisis of 1950 led to the production of synthetic heads.

LEFT A group of cloth dolls by the British maker Helene McLeod, produced in the 1980s. She is most well known for her African and Asian figures.

RIGHT The Christian Family Service Centre in China produced these two cloth dolls for sale in Hong Kong in the early twentieth century.

Lenci dolls

Lenci dolls are to Italy what Käthe Kruse dolls are to Germany. They are characterised by their all-felt heads and bodies with articulated limbs, painted features and exquisitely-designed felt clothes. The faces were moulded with realistic child-like expressions, with chubby cheeks. Some of the child dolls have cross expressions; some are girl or lady dolls, their faces painted with two-tone lips; their eyes often have two white dots added; some have real hair wigs and others mohair.

The popular belief that the two middle fingers of Lenci hands were stitched together is erroneous: some are like this but others have only stitched finger definition.

Because of the commercial success of Lenci dolls there were many copies at the time. True Lencis are marked in numerous ways – with ink stamps, card tags, ribbon labels and metal tags – the earliest being the metal tag. After 1938, cardboard tags were used. The most highly prized Lenci dolls are those made between 1920 and 1930.

LEFT A Lenci doll, produced in Italy circa 1920. She has a stuffed felt body with the rather cheeky facial expression painted on.

ABOVE An American felt doll produced by R. John Wright Dolls Inc in the 1980s. Sophisticated modern techniques allow them to achieve a highly realistic effect. This doll represents The Little Prince, a character from a children's book.

ABOVE This uncut cut-out cloth doll came with the instruction to 'sew together and stuff with cotton batting and sawdust'. It was produced by the American designers Celia and Charity Smith circa 1889.

LEFT A cloth doll designed by Norah Wellings, while she worked for Chad Valley, of Birmingham, England, circa 1935. He was named the HMS Furious. These sailor dolls were sold as souvenirs on ocean liners.

Steiff dolls

Fräulein Margarete Steiff, Giengen, Württenburg,
Germany is best known for stuffed toy animals of
superior quality. Although she died in 1909, the firm
continued in the family and is still going today. Her dolls
were of felt, plush and velvet and were characterized by
a seam down the centre of the face (which gives a
rather odd appearance) and a button in the ears. Felt
head dolls were first made in 1894. Most were
character dolls which have become extremely hard to
find. Some have specially balanced feet enabling them to
stand up without support.

CHAPTER SEVEN

MODERN DOLLS —
MODERN MATERIALS

· · · ·

It is difficult to define the modern period for doll manufacture. Madame Alexander, Lenci and Steiff are still in production and their modern creations are much collected. Firms such as Arranbee were in operation in the United States from 1922 until the 1960s. Mattel Inc.'s Barbie and Ken are a source of renewed interest for the modern doll and bring us into the age of hard plastics and vinyl. Dewees Cochran of California is a modern manufacturer of latex dolls, signed under the arm or behind the ear. The Ideal Novelty & Toy Co. of Brooklyn is another well-known American name.

'Effanbee' is the trademark of another well-known American doll manufacturer, Fleischaker & Baum. The company was founded in 1910 by Bernard E. Fleischaker and Hugo Baum. During the first few years, Effanbee produced 'Unbreakable' composition dolls and by 1918 it had added stuffed-body dolls to its range. In 1922, the 'They Walk and They Talk' line was introduced, and a year later the 'They Walk, They Talk, They

Sleep' dolls appeared. Baby Grumpy was introduced in 1914, and other favourites included Lovums (1918), Skippy (circa 1930), New Born Baby (1925) and the American Children series (1939).

The company also made historical dolls, portrait dolls and E f f a n b e e L i m i t e d Edition Dolls. It continues to make a wide range of dolls, but

LEFT A Japanese swimming doll made of celluloid circa 1920. Her arms flail in the water when the clockwork mechanism is wound up.

Pedigree Dolls and Toys Ltd (1938) of Canterbury, England, is another well-known English modern doll manufacturer. This was the first firm in England to make high-quality composition dolls. Among its products were period miniatures (1959) and story book dolls. But it is best-known today for Sindy, first produced in 1962, a teenage doll, 29cm (11½in) high, with a wonderful array of accessories.

the most keenly collected are those that were produced before the Second World War.

Barbie in the USA and Sindy in the UK were launched at the same time. They were the first modern fashion dolls. Sindy was the first doll to be advertised on television and she had a monopoly of the British market until 1980.

RIGHT This fine bisque model of Queen Elizabeth II was made by Peggy Nisbet in the 1970s to commemorate her coronation 25 years earlier.

Peggy Nisbet of Somerset, England, has become a specialist innovator in the art of the costume doll. She has produced such characters as Henry VIII and his wives, Mary Poppins, Christopher Robin and Pooh Bear. More recently, she produced a limited edition of 1,000 Prince Charles and Princess Diana wedding dolls, a limited edition set of Royal Children (Princess Diana with Prince William and Prince Harry) and a royal wedding collectors' limited edition set in hard styrene of Prince Andrew and Sarah Ferguson.

Palitoy, another big English manufacturer, brought out the popular Tiny Tears crying and wetting doll in the 1950s. However, the doll success story of the century is the Cabbage Patch doll, which has had record-breaking sales. The earliest examples are now collectors' items.

Trial and error

In spite of their apparent fragility, porcelain dolls have survived in considerable numbers, significantly more than dolls made of cloth, wood, wax and papier mâché, but the manufacturers were not satisfied, they wanted something more durable. Composition was quite successful, though not waterproof, but then celluloid came along. It was lightweight, waterproof, seemingly unbreakable, and could be planed, drilled, polished and moulded. Many doll-makers used it, but the early promise was not fulfilled. The dolls were easily squashed and once squashed, a celluloid doll's face never recovers its original shape; the colours faded and worse still, the dolls were inflammable.

Manufacturers also tried making rubber dolls. Again, rubber seemed the ideal – soft, unbreakable, paintable and mouldable. But the surface paint rubbed off and the rubber decomposed. In their turn, brass, zinc, copper, tin and aluminium were also used for doll's heads. Though some yielded attractive results, brass was heavy and the painted metal surface did not last well.

The precise date of the invention of hard plastic is difficult to establish, but by 1948 the Ideal Toy Co. of America was producing a well-finished doll with a hard plastic head with composition body and limbs, named Baby Coos. This was followed by Brother Coos and a

LEFT A rubber English Girl Guide doll made in the 1920s. Her paint has begun to peel. Rubber dolls continued to be made into the 1950s.

59

A new material girl – Barbie

By 1965 Mattel's Barbie and Ken, Fashion Queen Barbie and other dolls were all-vinyl. Barbie dolls, the original Teenage Fashion Models were the great phenomenon of 1959 and although Barbie lookalikes have come and gone, she remains queen of them all and is seriously collected and discussed in Barbie fan clubs. The great interest of collectors in these dolls has caused prices to rise considerably, so that a Barbie from the first production run is now worth over a thousand times what it cost to buy at the time. This much sought-after early model has holes in her feet lined with copper tubing that fits over the prongs of a black plastic stand, while subsequent dolls had wire stands that hooked under the arms.

The most dramatic changes in this doll have been in her hair. Starting with a pony tail, it changed to a bubble cut, then to straight hair in the 1970s and soft flowing tresses in the 1980s. The Fashion Queen Barbie came with moulded hair and three interchangeable wigs.

RIGHT These two Swiss dolls, dating from the 1920s, have jointed metal bodies and composition heads. The doll on the right is in full Edwardian dress.

Magic Skin Baby. Good quality, hard plastic wears well, but low-grade plastic splits or cracks at the seams.

RIGHT Cabbage Patch dolls were a phenomenon of the 1980s and had record-breaking sales for some time.

With the introduction of soft vinyl, manufacturers were able to make dolls with rooted wigs which could be washed, cut and styled. The dolls are also soft, unbreakable, washable and can be coloured realistically. The nature of the material enables fine-casting, so the dolls have plenty of realistic detail. They can, however, be stained with felt-tip or ballpoint pens.

Caring for plastic and vinyl dolls

Hard plastic dolls can easily be cleaned with detergent and water on a soft cloth, but it is best not to soak any doll, because the water may seep into the body. Vinyl is not biodegradeable and is impervious to decay and insects, but it can be damaged by mould which can stain.

Ballpoint pen is a common hazard and this too can be absorbed by vinyl and stain it. Working from the outer edge of the stain towards the centre, wash with a cloth soaked in an alcohol such as methylated spirits. Change the cloth as it becomes stained. Anything left will have penetrated the vinyl surface and you can try to remove this with hydrogen peroxide. Do not use bleach, acetone or ammonia.

ABOVE Superman was made by the MEGO Corp, Hong Kong in 1977. Action Man was made in England by Palitoy under licence from Hasbro in 1964.

From 1966 to 1986 one of the most popular playdolls was the English-made Sasha. This vinyl doll with a poseable body was produced in Stockport by the Friedland Doggart group to the designs of a Swiss artist named Sasha Morgenthaler. Her dolls have little facial modelling because she felt that a minimum indication of facial modelling on a doll was better than the excess of it usually found in commercially made dolls. The original Sasha dolls measured 51cm (20in) high and wore a wig of natural hair, while the factory-produced Sasha dolls made in England under the name Trendon are 41cm (16in) high and have rooted hair.

RIGHT A doll produced in the 1970s by General Mills, U.S.A. She has a hard plastic body and a vinyl head with a smiling mouth.

Living dolls

Modern dolls are tomorrow's collectables, if not already today's. The mechanical gimmicks of the future will be light years away from those wonderful innovations loved by yesterday's children: the age of the microchip and the computer may revolutionize doll collecting, but what materials will be used is hard to imagine. We have already trodden a long road to Palitoy's Tiny Tears or Mattel's Cheerful Tearful with its changing expressions. Many of today's children find it hard to relate to yesterday's playthings, just as the children of tomorrow may not relate to the toys of today. It is left to the collector to bridge the generations so that tomorrow's children may at least have an awareness and understanding of their past through the toys that earlier generations loved.

MUSEUMS, DEALERS AND FAIRS

● ● ● ●

Museums

UNITED STATES

Adirondack Center Museum, Court St., Elizabeth-town NY 12932

Alfred P. Sloan Museum, 1121 E. Kearsley St., Flint, MI 48503

Anita's Doll Museum & Boutique, 6737 Vesper Ave., Van Nuys, CA 91405

Antique Doll Museum, 1721 Broadway, Galveston, TX

Aunt Lens Doll & Toy Museum, 6 Hamilton Terrace, New York, NY 10031

Brooklyn Children's Museum, 145 Brooklyn Ave., Brooklyn, NY 11213

Cameron's Doll & Carriage Museum, 218 Becker's Lane, Manitou Springs, CO 80829

Camp McKensie Doll Museum, Mudo, SD 57559

Children's Museum, 3000 N. Meridian St., Indianapolis, IN 46206

Children's Museum, 300 Congress St., Boston, MA 02210

Children's Museum, 67 E. Kirbey, Detroit, MI 48202

Cotonlandia Museum, P. O. Box 1635, Greenwood, MS 38930

Cupids Bow Doll Museum, 958 Cambridge Ave., Sunnyvale, CA 94087

Diminutive Doll Domain, Box 757, Indian Brook Rd., Greene, NY 13778

Disney Dolls Museum, Grand Lake 'O the Cherokees, Disney, OK 74340

Doll Cabinet & Museum, Star Rt., Box 221, Ferriday, LA 71334

Doll Castle Doll Museum, 37 Belvedere Ave., Washington, NJ 07882

Doll Museum & Trading Post, Highway 30, Legrand, VA 50142

Doll Museum at Anne Le Ceglis, 5000 Calley, Norfolk, VA 23508

Dolls Den & Museum, 406 River Ave., Point Pleasant, Beach, NJ 08742

Dolls in Wonderland, 9 King Street, St. Augustine, FL 32084

1840 Doll House Museum, 196 Whitfield, Guilford, CT 06437

Enchanted World Doll Museum, Sioux Falls, South Dakota

Essie's Doll Museum, Rt. 16, Beech Bend Rd., Bowling Green, KY 42101,

Fairbanks Doll Museum, Hall Rd. (off Rt. 131), Sturbridge, MA

Fairhaven Doll Museum, 384 Alden Rd., Fairhaven, MA 02719

Gay 90's Button & Doll Museum, Rt. 1, Box 78, Eureka Springs, AR 72632

Gerwecks Doll Museum, 6299 Dixon Rd., Monroe, MI 48161

Geuther's Doll Museum, 188 N. Main St., Eureka Springs, AR 72632

Good Fairy Doll Museum, 205 Walnut Ave., Cranford, NJ 07016

Heirloom Doll Hospital/Shop/Museum, 416 E. Broadway, Waukesha, WI 53186

Helen Moe Antique Doll Museum, Hwy. 101 and Wellsona Rd., Paso Robles, CA 93446

Hobby Horse Doll/Toy Museum, 5310 Junius, Dallas, TX 78214

Hornosassa Doll Museum, Rt. 5, Box 145, Homosassa, FL 32646

Jacksonville Doll Museum, 5th & California St., Jacksonville, OR 97530

Jonaires Doll & Toy Museum, Rt. 4, Box 4476, Stroudsburg, PA 18360

Lolly's Doll & Toy Museum, 225 Magazine St., Galena, IL 61036

Madame Alexander's Doll Museum, 711 S. 3rd Ave., Chatsworth, GA 30705

Margaret Woodbury Strong Museum, 1 Manhattan Square, Rochester, NY 14607

McCurdy Historical Doll Museum, 246 N. 100 East, Prove. UT 84601

Memory Lane Doll & Toy Museum, Old Mystic Village, Mystic, CT 06355

Mary Merritt Doll Museum, Rt. 2, Douglassville, PA 19518

Museum of Antique Dolls, 505 E. President St., Savannah, GA 31401

Museum of Collectable Dolls, 1117 S. Florida Ave., Lakeland, FL 33803

Christine's Doll Museum, 4940 E. Speedway, Tucson, AZ 85712

Museums continued

Old Brown House Doll Museum, 1421 Ave. F, Cothenburg, NE 69138

Playhouse Museum of Old Dolls & Toys, 1201 N. 2nd St., Las Cruces, NM 88005

Poor Doll's Shop Museum, RR 2, Box 58, Syracuse, IN 46567

Society of Memories Doll Museum, 813 N. 2nd St., St. Joseph, MO 64502

Storybook Museum, 620 Louis St., Kerrville, TX 78028

Thomas County Museum, 1525 W. 4th St., Colby, KS 67701

Time Was Village Museum, Rt. 51, Mendota, IL 61342

Town of Yorktown Museum & Shop, 1974 Commerce St., Yorktown Heights, NY 10598

Toy Museum of Atlanta, 2800 Peachtree Rd., N.E., Atlanta, GA 30305

Treasure House Doll Museum, 1215 W. Will Rogers, Claremore, OK 74017

Victorian Doll Museum, 4332 Buffalo Rd., Rt. 33, Rochester, NY 14514

Washington Dolls' House Museum, 5236 44th St. NW Washington, DC 20015

Wenham Historical Museum, 132 Main St., Wenham, MA 01984

Yesteryears Doll Museum, Main & Diver St., Sandwich, MA 02563

ENGLAND

Arreton Manor, Arreton, Newport, Isle of Wight

Bath Museum of Costume, Assembly Rooms, Alfred St., Bath

Bethnal Green Museum of Childhood, Cambridge Heath Rd., London E2

Birmingham City Museums and Art Gallery, Congrave St., Birmingham

Blaise Castle Folk Museum, Henbury, Bristol BSIO 7QS

The Bowes Museum, Barnard Castle, Co. Durham

Cambridge and County Folk Museum, Castle St., Cambridge

The Castle Museum, York

The Gallery of English Costume, Platt Hall, Rusholme, Manchester

The London Toy & Model Museum, Craven Hill, London W2

Pollock's Toy Museum, 1 Scala St., London W1

Victoria & Albert Museum, South Kensington, London SW7

SCOTLAND

The Museum of Childhood, 42 High St., Edinburgh EHI ITB, Scotland

WALES

Penrhyn Castle Museum, Bangor

The Welsh Folk Museum, St. Fagan's, Cardiff

DENMARK

Leggoland Museum, Copenhagen

FRANCE

Musee Carnavalet, Paris

Musée des Arts Décoratifs, Paris

WEST GERMANY

Bavarian National Museum, Munich

Germanic National Museum, Kornmankt 1, Nuremberg

HOLLAND

Open Air Folk Museum, Arnhern

MONACO

Musée Nationale, Mme Gallea's Collection, Monte Carlo

SWEDEN

Swedish Museum, Djurgården, Stockholm

Dealers and Fairs

Chelsea Lion, c/o Chenil Gallery, 181–183 Kings Road, London SW3, England

Cohen Auctions, P.O. Box 425 – Rtes. 20–22, New Lebanon, NY 12125, USA

Confederate Dollers, P.O. Box 24485, New Orleans, LA 70124, USA

Grannies Goodies, P.O. Box 734, Forest Hill, London SE23, England

Helen Harten, Red Door Antiques, Prescott, AZ 86031, USA

Jackie Kaner, 9420 Reseda Blvd., Northridge, CA 91325, USA

Kimport Dolls, P.C. Box 495, Independence, MO 64051, USA

The London International Antique Dolls, Toys, Miniatures and Teddy Bear Fair, P.C. Box 734, Forest Hill, London SE23, England